How To Start A Coffee Business

Comprehensive Guide to Launching Your Own Coffee Shop from Scratch

Fitzpatrick J. Thompkins

Copyright © 2024 by **Fitzpatrick J. Thompkins**
All rights reserved

No part of this publication may be reproduced, stored in a retrieval system, or transmitted, in any form or by any means, electronic, mechanical, photocopying, recording, or otherwise, without the prior written permission of the author.

The information in this ebook is true and complete to the best of our knowledge. All recommendation are made without guarantee on the part of author or publisher. The author and publisher disclaim any liability in connection with the use of this information.

Table of Contents

Introduction   6
    Why Start a Coffee Business?   9
    Understanding the Coffee Industry: Trends and Growth   12

Chapter 1: Conceptualizing Your Coffee Business   14
    Choosing Your Coffee Business Model   14
    Creating a Unique Selling Proposition (USP)   17
    Market Research: Knowing Your Audience   20

Chapter 2: Business Planning   23
    Writing a Business Plan   23
    Setting Up Business Goals and Objectives   27
    Financial Planning   30

Chapter 3: Legal and Regulatory Compliance   33
    Choosing the Right Business Structure   33
    Necessary Licenses and Permits   36
    Health Regulations and Compliance   39

Chapter 4: Location and Setup   42
    Selecting the Ideal Location   42
    Design and Layout of Your Coffee Shop   45
    Purchasing Equipment   48
    Choosing Suppliers and Vendors   51

Chapter 5: Sourcing and Supply Chain Management   54
    Understanding Coffee Beans: Types and Origins   54
    Building Relationships with Suppliers   57
    Sustainability in Sourcing   60

Chapter 6: Branding and Marketing   63
    Developing Your Brand Identity   63
    Effective Marketing Strategies   66
    Building a Customer Base   69

Chapter 7: Operations Management   72
    Daily Operations and Workflow   72
    Staffing: Hiring and Training   75
    Quality Control and Customer Service   79

Chapter 8: Scaling Your Business   82
    Strategies for Growth and Expansion   82
    Franchising Opportunities   85
    Diversifying Your Product Offerings   88

Chapter 9: Financial Management   91
    Managing Finances: Accounting Basics   91
    Pricing Strategies   94
    Profit Maximization Tips   97

Chapter 10: Navigating Challenges   101
    Handling Competition   101
    Crisis Management   104
    Adapting to Market Changes   107

Chapter 11: The Future of Coffee Business   110
    Innovations in Coffee   110
    The Role of Technology   113
    Predictions and Preparations for Future Trends   116

Conclusion   119

Introduction

In the center of Seattle downtown, nestled among towering office buildings, a modest yet inviting coffee shop called "Espresso Dreams" buzzed with the warmth of freshly brewed coffee and the murmur of contented patrons. Behind the counter, Tom, the owner, prepared a cappuccino with practiced ease, his movements fluid and sure. It hadn't always been this way. Just two years ago, Tom had been a different person—a corporate drone trapped in a cubicle, dreaming of entrepreneurship.

Tom's journey from corporate monotony to the thriving owner of "Espresso Dreams" was nothing short of a revelation, sparked by a pivotal moment when he stumbled upon a book titled "How To Start A Coffee Business". As he now prepared a drink for a curious customer who seemed interested in his success story, he couldn't help but share how this book had been his guide.

"Why this book?" the customer asked, intrigued by Tom's enthusiastic endorsement.

Tom smiled, handing over the steaming cup. "Let me tell you a story," he began. "Two years ago, I was exactly where you are—curious and eager, but unsure where to begin. This book was my starting point. It didn't just teach me about coffee; it taught me how to build a business that reflects who I am."

He leaned closer, his voice tinged with excitement. "Each chapter was a step forward. From understanding the types of coffee businesses—like cafes, carts, and roasteries—to detailed business planning and financial management, the book laid out everything in a way that was easy to understand and apply."

Seeing the customer's interest deepen, Tom continued, "It covered legal aspects, like obtaining the right permits and choosing a business structure, which saved me from many potential legal headaches. It also dived into the nuances of selecting a location, designing a welcoming space, and even the intricate process of sourcing high-quality beans sustainably."

Tom's eyes sparkled as he gestured around his coffee shop. "Look around. The unique branding and interior design that you see? Inspired by strategies from the book. And the digital marketing that helped you find us today? That was all there too."

The customer nodded, visibly impressed. "It sounds comprehensive," he remarked.

"Oh, it is," Tom agreed. "But what's really great about it is how it prepares you for the real challenges. It talks about handling competition, managing finances, and even scaling the business. There's a whole chapter on navigating challenges that helped me through a tough first year."

As more customers queued up, Tom concluded, "This book isn't just a guide; it's the mentor I had when I was in your shoes. If you're seriously considering entering the coffee industry, I couldn't recommend it enough. It's practical, insightful, and, most importantly, it works. I'm living proof of that."

The customer, now holding the book in his hands, gave a thoughtful nod. "I'll take one copy. And another one of these excellent cappuccinos, please."

Tom chuckled, his heart swelling with pride as he turned back to the espresso machine. Each cup he brewed was a testament to his journey, a journey made possible by a book that had taught him not just to make coffee, but to make a difference.

Why Start a Coffee Business?

Starting a coffee business appeals to entrepreneurs for several reasons, ranging from the widespread popularity of coffee to the cultural significance that coffee shops hold in communities across the globe. Coffee remains one of the most consumed beverages in the world, with millions relying on it daily for a boost of energy. This steady demand creates a lucrative market opportunity for new business owners.

Venturing into the coffee industry allows for a variety of business models, from quaint cafes that serve as community hubs to mobile coffee carts catering to busy pedestrians in urban areas or private events. Each model offers flexibility and creativity in terms of scale, menu offerings, and customer engagement strategies. This versatility ensures that entrepreneurs can find a niche that suits their interests, budget, and local consumer behavior.

Another compelling reason to start a coffee business is the relatively low barrier to entry compared to other food and beverage ventures. For instance, a small coffee cart or a pop-up coffee stand requires minimal initial investment but still has the potential to generate significant revenue. Additionally, coffee businesses can be highly scalable. Owners can start small and expand gradually, opening multiple locations or even franchising their concept once they have established a successful business model and brand.

Moreover, coffee shops often become integral parts of their neighborhoods, providing a space where people can meet, work, and socialize. In today's fast-paced world, these businesses offer a comforting sense of community and continuity. The social aspect of a coffee business can be incredibly rewarding for owners who enjoy interacting with their customers and becoming a central part of their daily lives.

Furthermore, the coffee industry is ripe for innovation, allowing entrepreneurs to experiment with different coffee beans, brewing techniques, and drink recipes. The rise in consumer interest in sustainable and ethically sourced coffee products also presents an opportunity to cater to a niche market that values environmental and social responsibility.

Lastly, owning a coffee business can be personally rewarding. It provides a creative outlet and a chance to share a passion for coffee with others. It also offers a flexible lifestyle and the potential for financial independence. For those with a strong business plan and a commitment to quality, the coffee industry offers robust potential for success and satisfaction.

In sum, starting a coffee business offers numerous advantages, including high consumer demand, a variety of accessible business models, community engagement, opportunities for innovation, and personal fulfillment. These factors make it an attractive venture for aspiring entrepreneurs looking to make their mark in the food and beverage industry.

Understanding the Coffee Industry: Trends and Growth

The coffee industry has seen remarkable growth and shifts in trends that are essential to understand for anyone looking to start a coffee business. As one of the most beloved beverages worldwide, coffee presents a lucrative market opportunity, characterized by evolving consumer preferences and technological advancements.

Globally, the demand for coffee continues to rise, driven by increasing consumption in traditional markets like the United States and Europe, and significant growth in emerging markets such as China and India. This rising demand is coupled with a growing appreciation for specialty coffees, which have paved the way for a new wave of coffee shops and roasteries that focus on craft and quality. These establishments often source beans directly from farms, highlighting the importance of sustainability and ethical sourcing in today's market.

Consumer preferences are also shifting towards more unique and personalized coffee experiences. This trend is evident in the popularity of single-origin coffees and the rise of home brewing methods, such as pour-over and cold brew, which offer a deeper appreciation of the coffee's flavor profile. Additionally, health-conscious consumers are increasingly drawn to alternatives like decaffeinated and plant-based milk-infused coffees, influencing product offerings in coffee shops.

Technological advancements play a critical role in shaping the coffee industry. From the farm to the coffee cup, innovations such as precision agriculture, blockchain for traceability, and automated espresso machines enhance efficiency and quality. These technologies not only improve farming practices but also enhance the customer experience by enabling cafes to produce consistently high-quality coffee at greater speeds.

The business landscape of the coffee industry is also evolving. There is a noticeable shift towards digital platforms for marketing and sales. Coffee shops and roasteries increasingly leverage social media to build their brand and engage with customers directly. E-commerce platforms are becoming essential for coffee businesses, allowing them to expand their reach beyond local markets and cater to a global audience.

Understanding these trends and the overall growth of the coffee industry is crucial for new entrants. It provides them with the knowledge needed to make informed decisions about their business model, product offerings, and marketing strategies. With the industry's dynamic nature, keeping abreast of these changes can significantly impact the success of a new coffee business, positioning it well within a competitive and ever-growing market.

Chapter 1: Conceptualizing Your Coffee Business

Choosing Your Coffee Business Model

Choosing the right business model is a critical decision for anyone venturing into the coffee industry, as it sets the foundation for your operations, branding, and financial structure. There are several models to consider, each with its unique attributes and challenges.

Coffee Shop

One of the most popular choices is opening a coffee shop. This model is all about creating a welcoming atmosphere where customers can enjoy high-quality coffee and perhaps some light snacks or pastries. Success in this model hinges on location, ambiance, and quality. A coffee shop needs to be accessible and inviting to attract steady foot traffic. Design elements like comfortable seating, appealing decor, and free Wi-Fi can enhance customer experience and increase dwell time. Additionally, offering a variety of coffee options, including specialty and seasonal brews, can help differentiate your coffee shop in a competitive market.

Coffee Cart

For entrepreneurs with limited capital, a coffee cart can be an excellent entry point into the coffee business. This model offers mobility and lower startup costs than a traditional brick-and-mortar coffee shop. Coffee carts can operate in multiple locations such as parks, events, or busy downtown areas, catering to morning commuters or event-goers. The key to success with a coffee cart is selecting the right locations where high foot traffic is likely, and there is a demand for quick, convenient access to quality coffee.

Roastery
Starting a coffee roastery allows you to source, roast, and sell your coffee beans. This model appeals to those interested in the craft of coffee and who want control over the flavor profile of the beans they sell. Roasteries can supply coffee to businesses and individual consumers, offering unique blends or single-origin beans that are ethically sourced. This business model requires more knowledge about coffee processing and may involve a larger upfront investment in roasting equipment. However, it also offers higher margins and the potential for wholesale distribution.

Franchise
Buying into a coffee franchise can be appealing because it provides a ready-made business model along with brand recognition and support from the franchisor. Franchises may offer training, operational guidelines, and marketing support, which can be particularly beneficial for first-time business owners. However, it's

important to consider that franchisees often have less creative control and are required to make ongoing royalty payments. The success of a franchise largely depends on the strength of the brand and the location of the outlet.

Each coffee business model has distinct advantages and requires different levels of investment and expertise. When choosing your model, consider your financial resources, business goals, market research, and personal interests in the coffee industry. Understanding your target market's preferences and how they align with each business model can also guide your decision. Whether creating a cozy spot for coffee lovers to gather, hitting the streets with a mobile cart, delving into the art of roasting, or leveraging an established brand, your choice will pave the way for your business's unique identity and market position.

Creating a Unique Selling Proposition (USP)

Creating a Unique Selling Proposition (USP) is a fundamental step in conceptualizing any business, especially in a competitive market like the coffee industry. A USP defines what makes your business distinct from competitors, highlighting attributes that appeal specifically to your target audience. For aspiring coffee shop owners, crafting a compelling USP is not just about serving coffee—it involves creating an experience or offering that can't be found elsewhere.

First, consider the core of what a coffee business can offer—this could range from unique flavors and brewing techniques to an exceptional atmosphere. It's important to think beyond just the product (coffee) and consider how the service, environment, and overall brand feel contribute to the USP. For example, a coffee shop might differentiate itself by using exclusively organic, locally sourced coffee beans, thus appealing to environmentally conscious consumers. Alternatively, it could offer a highly tech-driven service, like app-based ordering and customization, appealing to tech-savvy urbanites.

The location and design of the coffee shop also play critical roles in shaping the USP. A coffee shop in a bustling downtown area might focus on speed and convenience to cater to busy professionals, while one located in a more relaxed setting might emphasize comfort, offering plush seating and a calm atmosphere ideal for studying or meetings.

Another aspect to consider is the customer experience. This includes not only the physical interaction with the space and the product but also the emotional and psychological aspects. Creating a strong community presence, with events like live music nights, poetry readings, or coffee brewing classes, can significantly enhance a coffee shop's appeal. These activities not only make the business stand out but also help in building a loyal customer base.

Moreover, sustainability can be a powerful USP in today's market, where consumers are increasingly aware of environmental issues. This could involve several practices like minimizing waste, using compostable cups, supporting fair trade practices, and promoting recycling. Communicating these efforts effectively can make your coffee shop particularly attractive to a growing segment of environmentally aware patrons.

Finally, integrating technology can further refine your USP. From sophisticated point-of-sale systems that streamline operations to offering free Wi-Fi and outlets for laptops, technology can enhance customer convenience and satisfaction, making your coffee shop a preferred destination for both work and relaxation.

In crafting your USP, it's essential to conduct thorough market research to understand what competitors are offering and identify gaps in the market. Engage with potential customers through surveys or informal conversations to gain insights into their needs and preferences. This information will be invaluable as you define what makes your coffee shop unique.

In conclusion, a USP is not just a marketing tool, but a strategic framework that guides every decision in your business—from the design of your shop and the type of products you offer to the way you interact with customers. It's about carving out a niche in a competitive industry and consistently delivering on your promise to customers, ensuring they not only visit once but become regular patrons.

Market Research: Knowing Your Audience

Conducting thorough market research is an indispensable step when conceptualizing your coffee business, allowing you to understand the preferences, behaviors, and needs of your target audience. This deep dive into your potential customer base informs everything from the location and design of your coffee shop to the types of products you offer and the marketing strategies you employ.

Starting with demographic analysis is crucial. This involves identifying the age, gender, income levels, and lifestyle choices of your potential customers. For example, a coffee shop in a bustling city business district might cater to professionals seeking quick, high-quality brews and a place for informal meetings. Conversely, a location near a university might focus on affordable options and a comfortable setting conducive for studying and socializing.

Beyond demographics, psychographic information, which includes values, attitudes, interests, and lifestyles, plays a critical role. Understanding whether your customers value eco-friendly practices can influence your decision to source organic coffee and offer biodegradable cups. Similarly, recognizing a trend towards health-consciousness might prompt you to include sugar-free and alternative milk options on your menu.

Geographic considerations also affect your market understanding. The local climate can influence the types of coffee products favored; colder regions might see higher sales in hot drinks and vice versa. Additionally, the cultural significance of coffee in the location you choose can impact consumer behavior—areas with a strong coffee culture might value single-origin beans and artisanal brewing techniques more highly.

Behavioral data is another pillar of market research, highlighting consumption patterns such as peak buying times and the popularity of different coffee types. Observing and analyzing the frequency of purchases and the preference for take-away versus dine-in can help tailor your operational strategies effectively.

Competitive analysis is equally important. Identifying and studying competitors helps you find a niche or an under-served segment of the market. It can also offer insights into successful business practices and common pitfalls in the local coffee scene. This knowledge assists in differentiating your business through unique selling propositions, be it superior customer service, innovative product offerings, or a compelling loyalty program.

Lastly, engaging directly with your potential market through surveys, focus groups, and feedback on social media can provide invaluable insights. These interactions can reveal what customers think about your concept, what they feel is missing in the current market, and how well your proposed offerings might meet their expectations.

By systematically gathering and analyzing this varied information, you can build a robust foundation for your coffee business. This research not only helps in making informed decisions but also significantly enhances your ability to attract and retain customers, ultimately contributing to the success and sustainability of your venture.

Chapter 2: Business Planning

Writing a Business Plan

Writing a business plan is a fundamental step in starting any business, including a coffee shop. This document serves not only as a roadmap for the business's development and operation but also as a tool to attract investors and secure financing. For a coffee business, the business plan must reflect a deep understanding of the coffee industry, including market trends, customer demographics, and competitive strategies.

The business plan should start with a clear executive summary, which outlines the key aspects of the coffee business such as the business concept, essential financial information, and what sets it apart from the competition. This section is crucial as it often determines whether an investor will be interested enough to read further.

Following the executive summary, the business plan should detail the business's objectives. These should be specific, measurable, achievable, relevant, and time-bound (SMART). Objectives for a coffee shop might include achieving a certain revenue target, opening additional locations within a certain number of years, or achieving a specific amount of sustainable or ethically sourced coffee sales.

The next section should be a market analysis. Here, the owner needs to provide research on the coffee industry at both local and national levels. This analysis should include information on current market trends, such as the increasing popularity of specialty coffees or the rise of mobile ordering and delivery services. Additionally, it should analyze direct and indirect competitors, highlighting what the new coffee shop will do differently or better. This could involve a focus on niche markets, such as organic coffees or vegan café options.

The business structure section should outline the legal structure of the coffee business. Will it operate as a sole proprietorship, a partnership, or a corporation? The decision impacts tax obligations, liability, and the business's ability to raise money.

A critical part of the business plan is the section detailing the business model. This should explain how the coffee shop will make money. Typical revenue streams in a coffee business include beverage sales (coffee, teas, other beverages), food items, merchandise, and sometimes subscription services or specialty training and workshops. This section should also cover pricing strategy, which must be competitive yet sufficient to cover costs and generate profit.

Operations and management plans are also vital. This section should describe the day-to-day operations of the coffee shop, including sourcing of coffee, staffing, customer service, and inventory management. It should detail the roles and responsibilities of the management team, highlighting their skills and experience as relevant to the success of the coffee business.

Marketing and sales strategies come next. This part should focus on how the coffee shop will attract and retain customers. Strategies may include social media marketing, loyalty programs, community events, and promotions. It should clearly outline the brand messaging, key marketing channels, and sales tactics that will be used to achieve the business objectives.

Financial projections are another essential element. This section should include detailed forecasts for income, cash flow, and expenditure. These projections should be based on realistic assumptions about growth in customer numbers and average spend per customer. Including best-case and worst-case scenarios can help demonstrate that the business is viable under various conditions.

Finally, a risk analysis should be conducted to identify potential challenges the coffee business might face and propose strategies to mitigate these risks. This could include anything from unexpected supplier price hikes to changes in consumer preferences or economic downturns.

Overall, the business plan for a coffee shop must be comprehensive, well-researched, and realistic. It should provide a clear picture of how the business will be created, run, and grown, serving as a living document that evolves along with the business.

Setting Up Business Goals and Objectives

Setting up business goals and objectives is a crucial step in the business planning process, especially for aspiring entrepreneurs in the coffee industry. Clear goals and objectives not only provide a roadmap for launching and growing a coffee business but also help in measuring success and making informed decisions.

When starting a coffee business, the first objective should be to define what success looks like. This could be financial stability, brand recognition, customer loyalty, or a combination of these elements. Financial goals are typically quantifiable, such as achieving a specific annual revenue, maintaining profit margins, or reaching a break-even point within a certain time frame. These financial objectives need to be realistic, considering factors like startup costs, ongoing expenses, and expected revenue from sales.

Apart from financial targets, setting qualitative goals is equally important. This might include becoming a well-known local coffee spot, being recognized for sustainability practices, or becoming the preferred choice among coffee aficionados in the community. These goals are generally more subjective but can be measured through customer feedback, online reviews, and brand visibility in the market.

Objectives should also focus on operational excellence, such as ensuring that the coffee shop operates efficiently, the quality of the coffee and customer service is consistently high, and that the business adheres to regulatory standards. For instance, an objective could be to serve customers within a specific time frame from ordering or to maintain a customer satisfaction rate of over 90%.

Another critical set of objectives revolves around market penetration and growth. For a new coffee business, initial goals might include capturing a certain percentage of the local market share or establishing a set number of loyal customers within the first year. Long-term objectives could aim at expanding the business through additional outlets or scaling up operations to include online sales and home deliveries.

Innovation should also be part of the business objectives. This could involve regularly introducing new coffee blends, adopting emerging coffee brewing technologies, or creating seasonal promotional campaigns. The aim is to keep the business dynamic and competitive in a market that values novelty and quality.

Setting objectives for sustainability practices is increasingly important. Objectives may include measures to reduce waste, use of biodegradable packaging, or sourcing beans from fair-trade certified farms. These practices not only contribute to environmental conservation but also appeal to a growing segment of consumers who value ethical and sustainable business practices.

To effectively manage and achieve these goals, it is essential to break them down into actionable steps. Each objective should have a timeline and be assigned to specific team members to ensure accountability. Regular reviews and adjustments should also be part of the process, as the business environment and consumer preferences can change rapidly.

In sum, when setting up business goals and objectives for a coffee business, it is crucial to be clear, specific, and realistic. These goals should guide daily operations, influence strategic decisions, and align with the overall vision and mission of the business. They serve as a foundation for the business plan and are essential for securing funding, managing growth, and achieving long-term success.

Financial Planning

Financial planning is a cornerstone of success for any business, and starting a coffee business is no exception. It involves a systematic approach to setting up your financial structure, budgeting effectively, and securing the necessary funding to support your business from inception through its growth stages.

Starting a coffee business requires a clear understanding of the initial capital needed to launch effectively. This includes costs related to leasing or purchasing a space, renovations and decor to create a welcoming atmosphere, purchasing equipment like espresso machines and grinders, and initial inventory such as coffee beans, milk, sugar, and other essentials. Additionally, operational costs such as utilities, payroll, insurance, and marketing must be considered in the financial plan.

Creating a detailed business plan is critical as it provides a blueprint of your expected revenue and expenses. This plan should outline all startup costs, projected cash flow, and break-even analysis. It helps in understanding how much money the business needs to start and operate until it becomes profitable, which is crucial for maintaining liquidity and operational stability.

Budgeting is another critical component. It involves allocating financial resources to different areas of the business to maximize cost-efficiency without compromising on quality or customer service. Effective budgeting will help control expenditures, forecast monthly spending, and prepare for unforeseen expenses that might arise.

Funding the venture can come from various sources. Personal savings are often the first option for many entrepreneurs, but additional funds might be required to fully establish the business. This can be obtained through small business loans, which are offered by many banks and financial institutions with varying terms and interest rates that need to be carefully compared. Investors, such as angel investors or venture capitalists, provide another avenue for funding. They not only bring in money but might also offer valuable guidance and business connections. Crowdfunding through platforms like Kickstarter or GoFundMe has also become a popular method to raise funds, especially for businesses with a compelling story or unique concept.

Managing the finances of a coffee shop does not end with the initial setup. It extends to daily operations, where effective financial management involves regular monitoring of cash flow, adjusting budgets as necessary, and ensuring that the business remains profitable. It also includes managing taxes and compliance with financial regulations, which can significantly affect the bottom line.

Furthermore, as the business grows, reinvestment becomes crucial. Profits might be channeled back into the business to expand product lines, enhance the store environment, or open new locations. Financial planning for growth must be strategic and based on sound market analysis to ensure that expansions contribute to increased profitability without overextending the company's resources.

In conclusion, financial planning for a coffee business is a multifaceted process that encompasses a range of activities from initial budgeting and securing funds to ongoing financial management and strategic growth planning. It requires a thorough understanding of both the immediate financial needs and the long-term financial strategies that will help the business thrive in a competitive marketplace.

Chapter 3: Legal and Regulatory Compliance

Choosing the Right Business Structure

Choosing the right business structure is a critical decision when starting a coffee business, as it impacts everything from your day-to-day operations to your taxes, and how much your personal assets are at risk. The structure you choose influences your ability to grow the business, your formal requirements, and your liabilities. Understanding each type of business structure and selecting the right one can save you time, money, and headaches.

For small coffee shop owners, the most common structures include sole proprietorship, partnership, limited liability company (LLC), and corporation. Each has its advantages and disadvantages, depending on the specific needs and goals of the business.

Sole Proprietorship is the simplest and most straightforward business structure. It's inexpensive to form and offers complete managerial control to the owner. However, the downside is that the owner is personally liable for all financial obligations of the business. This risk can be significant if the business incurs debt or faces lawsuits.

Partnership involves two or more people who agree to share in the profits or losses of a business. A major benefit is the pooling of resources and expertise, which can enhance the business's ability to secure funding and other needs. Similar to a sole proprietorship, partners usually face personal liability for the business debts and liabilities.

Limited Liability Company (LLC) is a more flexible option for small business owners, combining the benefits of both partnership and corporation structures. It provides limited liability protection to its owners, meaning personal assets are protected from business debts and claims. This structure is particularly advantageous for coffee shops because it shields the owner from personal liability in many instances while allowing the profits and losses of the business to be passed through to owners' personal income tax returns, avoiding double taxation.

Corporation offers the strongest protection from personal liability, but it is more costly to organize and involves more complex regulations and tax requirements. Corporations can raise funds through the sale of stock, which may be advantageous for those looking to expand. However, they are subjected to double taxation—first, at the corporate income level and again at the personal level on dividends. Small coffee shops rarely form as corporations due to the complexity and formal requirements involved, but it might be suitable for larger establishments planning aggressive expansion strategies.

When choosing a legal structure, it's also important to consider specific licensing requirements for a coffee shop, which can vary by location. Local health department regulations, business licenses, and permits for food service are typically necessary and can be influenced by the business structure chosen.

Moreover, the chosen business structure will determine which tax forms need to be filed. It's advisable to consult with a business accountant or attorney who understands the specific needs of a coffee business to ensure that your shop is compliant with federal, state, and local tax laws, which differ significantly among business structures.

Ultimately, the decision on which business structure to choose depends on a number of factors including the number of owners, the type of operations, the level of acceptable risk, and the financial goals of the business. By considering these factors, entrepreneurs can select a structure that not only minimizes liability and tax implications but also supports their business's growth and day-to-day operations.

Necessary Licenses and Permits

Starting a coffee business involves navigating various legal and regulatory requirements, including obtaining the necessary licenses and permits. These are critical to ensure that the business operates within the law, avoiding potential fines and legal issues.

Firstly, a basic business license, also known as a business operation license, is required for any entity engaging in commerce. This license signifies that the business is registered with the local government and is recognized as a legitimate entity. The specifics can vary widely depending on the location, including city, state, and country regulations, so it's essential to consult local government resources or a legal advisor to understand the precise requirements.

Beyond the basic business license, a coffee shop may also need a food service license, sometimes referred to as a food handler's permit. Since coffee shops serve food and beverages, this license is mandatory and ensures that the business adheres to health and safety regulations pertinent to food service establishments. Obtaining this license typically involves a health department inspection to verify that the premises meet all sanitary requirements, and employees may need to complete food safety training.

If the coffee shop plans to sell alcoholic beverages, an additional liquor license will be necessary. The process of obtaining a liquor license can be quite complex and expensive, involving strict scrutiny of the business and its operators. The requirements for this permit can also vary significantly by location, often influenced by local laws regarding alcohol sales.

Another essential permit for a coffee shop, especially if it involves the roasting of coffee beans, is an environmental permit. Roasting coffee can produce emissions that must be controlled and monitored under environmental protection laws. This permit ensures that the business complies with air quality standards and typically involves inspections and possibly restrictions on the types of equipment or fuels used.

In some areas, a signage permit might be required if the business plans to install any exterior signs. Local zoning laws often dictate the size, location, and sometimes the lighting of business signs. This permit helps maintain a certain aesthetic in the community and ensures that all signs are safe and do not obstruct public areas.

Lastly, if the coffee shop includes any construction or significant remodeling, a building permit will likely be necessary. This permit is to ensure that all construction complies with building codes, including fire safety, structural integrity, and accessibility. Often, this process requires submitting detailed construction plans and undergoing inspections during and after the construction phase.

Given the complexity and variability of these requirements, it is advisable for aspiring coffee shop owners to conduct thorough research and possibly consult with professionals specializing in business law and food service regulations. This preparation not only prevents legal complications but also contributes to a smoother launch and operation of the coffee business. Understanding and complying with these licensing and permitting requirements is foundational to establishing a legally compliant and successful coffee shop.

Health Regulations and Compliance

Starting a coffee business requires meticulous attention to health regulations and compliance to ensure the safety of both employees and customers, and to adhere to legal standards that govern food and beverage services. Compliance with these regulations not only protects the business from legal issues but also builds trust and credibility with customers.

Firstly, understanding local health codes is crucial. These regulations are primarily concerned with the safety, cleanliness, and overall operation of food and beverage establishments. Regulations typically cover a wide range of areas including food handling, storage, preparation, and employee hygiene. Each locality may have specific requirements, but generally, the goal is to prevent foodborne illnesses and ensure public health is not compromised.

Before opening a coffee shop, an owner must secure a health permit from local authorities, which involves an inspection by health officials. This inspection checks for proper sanitation, the correct use of equipment, adequate pest control, and employee health and hygiene practices. It's essential for business owners to be well-prepared for these inspections, ensuring that their establishment meets all required standards.

In addition to local health codes, there are federal regulations to consider, particularly those administered by the Food and Drug Administration (FDA) in the United States. These regulations pertain to the labeling of products, nutritional content disclosures, and the handling of allergens, which can be crucial for businesses that also serve food or sell packaged coffee beans.

Employee training is another critical component of complying with health regulations. Staff must be trained and certified in food safety practices, which include proper food handling techniques, understanding cross-contamination risks, and knowing the correct temperatures for storing and serving food and beverages. Many localities require that at least one staff member has a food safety certification, and maintaining these certifications involves regular courses and testing.

Compliance also extends to the design and maintenance of the premises. This includes ensuring that the layout of the coffee shop promotes good hygiene practices, with facilities such as handwashing stations readily accessible to employees. The materials used in the construction of food preparation areas, such as countertops and flooring, must be easy to clean and sanitize. Regular maintenance checks should be performed to ensure equipment is functioning correctly and safely.

Waste management is another important area. Coffee shops must have protocols for the disposal of waste materials, including food scraps and packaging, in ways that comply with local environmental and health regulations. Effective waste management practices help prevent issues related to pest infestations and unsanitary conditions.

Lastly, as coffee businesses often cater to a diverse clientele, including individuals with disabilities, compliance with the Americans with Disabilities Act (ADA) ensures that the business is accessible to all customers. This includes physical layout adjustments, appropriate signage, and potentially, service provisions for customers with special needs.

Overall, navigating the myriad of health regulations and compliance issues is vital for successfully starting and running a coffee business. It requires ongoing attention and adaptation to regulatory changes, which can sometimes be frequent. Ensuring compliance not only minimizes the risk of legal penalties but also enhances the reputation of the business, fostering a safe and welcoming environment for customers.

Chapter 4: Location and Setup

Selecting the Ideal Location

Selecting the ideal location is a pivotal decision in the process of starting a coffee business, as it significantly influences customer traffic, sales volume, and overall brand visibility. The right location can draw a steady stream of customers, while a poor choice can hinder even the most well-conceptualized coffee shops.

When considering locations, entrepreneurs should begin with a thorough analysis of their target market. Understanding who the customers are, including their habits, preferences, and demographics, helps in choosing a spot that aligns with their lifestyles. For instance, a coffee shop near a university might focus on affordable prices and fast service, catering to students, whereas one in a business district might prioritize high-quality brews and a space conducive for meetings.

Traffic patterns are also crucial. High foot traffic areas near public transport hubs, office buildings, or shopping centers offer natural customer flows. However, these areas might also come with higher rent, so it's important to balance the potential increase in sales with the overhead costs. Visibility from the street can enhance spontaneous visits, which are valuable in building a customer base.

Competition in the area is another important factor. Being near other coffee shops isn't always a negative; it can indicate a high demand for coffee in the area. However, it is vital to differentiate your offering to capture a share of the market. If the competition is too intense, consider a location with fewer direct competitors, or focus on a niche that is underrepresented in the area, such as organic or specialty brews.

The size and layout of the potential location must also be considered. The space should not only accommodate current needs but also allow for future growth. It should have a logical flow from the entrance to the order counter to the seating area, which enhances the customer experience. Additionally, there should be enough space for kitchen operations to run smoothly, including areas for food preparation, storage, and cooking if the menu extends beyond coffee.

Accessibility and convenience for customers are key. Locations with parking facilities, bike racks, or near public transportation are advantageous. Also, consider the ease of access for suppliers for efficient delivery and operations.

Lease terms and conditions can also impact the choice of location. Entrepreneurs should seek flexible lease terms to avoid being locked into a long-term commitment before understanding the full potential of the location. Negotiating a lease with options to renew can provide stability for the business once the location proves successful.

Lastly, compliance with zoning laws and local regulations is mandatory. Before signing a lease, ensure the space is zoned for a coffee shop and that there will be no legal issues with signage, renovations, or operations. Understanding these legalities in advance can save time, money, and frustration.

Selecting the right location is a mixture of art and science — it requires both analytical thinking to interpret market data and intuitive understanding of a place's potential to attract customers. A well-chosen location not only boosts the immediate likelihood of a coffee shop's success but also sets a strong foundation for its future growth.

Design and Layout of Your Coffee Shop

The design and layout of a coffee shop are crucial elements that contribute significantly to its success. This goes beyond mere aesthetics; it involves creating an environment that enhances customer experience, optimizes operational efficiency, and reflects the brand's identity.

When planning the design and layout of a coffee shop, the first consideration is the flow of traffic. This involves the arrangement of the entrance, counter, seating areas, and pathways to ensure a smooth flow of customers and staff. Efficient traffic flow helps prevent congestion and allows easy access to the counter and seating areas, which can enhance the customer experience by reducing wait times and creating a relaxed atmosphere.

The counter, where orders are placed and served, is the focal point of most coffee shops. It should be strategically positioned to be immediately visible upon entry, which helps in guiding customers effortlessly to place their orders. Behind the counter, the workspace must be ergonomically designed to allow baristas to move efficiently and safely, with easy access to espresso machines, grinders, and other tools. This setup not only speeds up service but also provides an engaging spectacle for customers, who often enjoy watching their beverages being crafted.

Seating is another critical aspect of coffee shop design. A variety of seating options should be provided to cater to different customer needs and preferences. Some patrons may prefer cozy, intimate spaces for lengthy stays, while others might need quick-access seating for brief visits. Including options like communal tables can encourage social interactions among customers, while quiet corners with comfortable chairs are perfect for those looking to work or read. The choice of furniture should reflect the coffee shop's branding and be designed for durability and comfort.

Lighting within a coffee shop plays a pivotal role in creating the right mood and ambiance. Natural light is highly prized for making spaces feel larger and more welcoming. Where natural light is limited, the choice of artificial lighting should be warm and inviting, avoiding overly bright or harsh lighting that can detract from the cozy atmosphere most coffee enthusiasts seek.

Aesthetics are intimately tied to the brand's identity. The choice of colors, materials, and decorations should align with the brand's theme and appeal to its target audience. For instance, a modern, minimalist coffee shop might feature clean lines and neutral colors, while a rustic-themed shop might opt for wood finishes and vintage decor. The design should also be adaptive to seasonal decorations and promotions without losing the brand's core visual identity.

Moreover, the design should consider practical elements such as power outlets for customers who might need to charge electronic devices, soundproofing materials to reduce noise pollution, and Wi-Fi infrastructure to ensure a strong and reliable internet connection. These factors significantly contribute to the comfort and convenience of customers, making them more likely to return.

Finally, sustainability practices in the design and layout can significantly impact customer perception. This can include the use of eco-friendly materials, energy-efficient appliances, and designs that maximize natural heating and cooling. Demonstrating a commitment to sustainability can not only reduce operational costs but also appeal to environmentally conscious consumers.

In summary, the design and layout of a coffee shop are not just about physical appearance but about creating a functional space that enhances customer experience, reflects the brand's identity, and operates efficiently. This comprehensive approach to design will help ensure that the coffee shop is a welcoming, comfortable, and attractive place for customers to enjoy their coffee.

Purchasing Equipment

Purchasing the right equipment is a critical step in setting up a successful coffee business. The quality of the equipment can significantly influence the efficiency of the coffee shop's operations and the quality of the coffee served. Therefore, making informed decisions during the purchasing process is essential for ensuring that the equipment meets both the current and future needs of the business.

When starting a coffee business, the first step in purchasing equipment is to identify the type of coffee shop and the menu offerings. This decision will dictate the kind of equipment required. For instance, a simple coffee cart might need a basic espresso machine and a small grinder, whereas a full-scale café would require several types of coffee machines, grinders, brewing systems, and possibly equipment for baking if pastries and snacks are on the menu.

The centerpiece of most coffee shops is the espresso machine, and choosing the right one is paramount. Factors to consider include the machine's capacity, the speed of service it can handle, its durability, and ease of use. High-quality espresso machines not only deliver better taste but also ensure reliability during peak hours. Brands that are well-known for durability and service can be more expensive but are usually worth the investment due to their longevity and lower maintenance costs.

Grinders are also vital as the grind size greatly affects the extraction process and the overall flavor of the coffee. Investing in a high-quality grinder can enhance the taste of the coffee, which can differentiate a coffee shop in a competitive market. It is advisable to choose grinders that allow for adjustments in grind size and consistency to cater to different brewing methods.

In addition to coffee machines and grinders, other essential equipment includes blenders for mixed beverages, commercial refrigerators for storing milk and cream, dishwashers for managing cleanliness, and ovens or toasters if the menu includes food items. Each piece of equipment should be selected based on capacity, space requirements, energy efficiency, and compatibility with the other tools in the shop.

For coffee shops focusing on sustainability, choosing equipment with energy-saving features is crucial. This not only reduces the shop's carbon footprint but also cuts down on utility costs. Energy-efficient espresso machines, grinders, and refrigerators are available in the market that perform at par with traditional equipment while using less energy.

Another consideration is the layout and space optimization in the coffee shop. The equipment should fit well within the designated space, allowing for an efficient workflow. Baristas should have easy access to everything they need to minimize movement and speed up service. Proper ventilation is also necessary, especially for equipment that emits heat.

Lastly, the purchasing process should include considering the after-sales service and warranty conditions. Equipment in a coffee shop undergoes significant wear and tear; hence, choosing brands that offer good customer service and have accessible repair services can prevent prolonged downtime, which could affect business operations.

By carefully selecting equipment that meets the specific needs of their business model, new coffee shop owners can ensure they are well-prepared to deliver high-quality service to their customers. This not only impacts the efficiency and the economics of the coffee shop but also plays a crucial role in defining the overall customer experience.

Choosing Suppliers and Vendors

Choosing the right suppliers and vendors is a critical step in the setup of a successful coffee business. The quality of the products and services provided by these partners can significantly affect the operation and reputation of your coffee shop. This selection process involves several key considerations, from the quality of the coffee beans to the reliability of equipment suppliers and the cost-effectiveness of each vendor.

Firstly, the selection of coffee bean suppliers is paramount. The origin and quality of the beans determine the flavor and uniqueness of the coffee you offer. It's essential to seek suppliers who source their beans ethically and sustainably, aligning with the increasing consumer demand for responsible business practices. Establishing direct trade relationships with coffee farmers can also be beneficial. This not only ensures the freshness and quality of the coffee but also supports the farming communities directly, which can be a strong marketing point.

Furthermore, considering the suppliers of coffee-related products such as syrups, pastries, and other consumables is equally important. These products should complement the quality of your coffee and enhance the overall customer experience. Opt for vendors who consistently meet food safety standards and deliver fresh and high-quality products.

The choice of equipment vendors is another crucial aspect. The efficiency, durability, and reliability of the coffee machines and grinders can impact your service speed and the quality of coffee served. It's advisable to select well-established vendors with proven track records who offer after-sales service and maintenance. This ensures that any disruptions in service due to equipment failure are minimized.

Additionally, the location of your suppliers and vendors plays a significant role in determining your inventory management strategy. Choosing local vendors can reduce delivery times and shipping costs, which is particularly important for perishable goods like pastries and dairy products. However, some specialized items, like high-quality coffee beans or specific coffee equipment, might need to be sourced from farther away, necessitating a more strategic approach to stock management.

Cost is always a consideration, but it should not be the sole factor in choosing suppliers and vendors. It's often worth paying a bit more for higher quality products and reliable service that can enhance your reputation and customer satisfaction. Moreover, establishing strong relationships with your suppliers can lead to better prices, higher quality goods, and favorable credit terms.

In summary, selecting the right suppliers and vendors for a coffee business involves balancing quality, cost, reliability, and ethical considerations. It requires thorough research and careful consideration of how each choice affects both the operation of the business and the customer experience. Successful coffee shop owners understand that their suppliers and vendors are indeed partners in their business, and choosing wisely can lead to mutual growth and success.

Chapter 5: Sourcing and Supply Chain Management

Understanding Coffee Beans: Types and Origins

In starting a coffee business, a deep understanding of coffee beans—their types and origins—is fundamental. This knowledge not only informs the quality of the product offered but also shapes the sourcing strategies and relationships within the supply chain.

Coffee beans are primarily of two types: Arabica and Robusta. Arabica beans are known for their smooth, complex flavor profiles, with varying degrees of acidity and often a hint of sweetness. They are predominantly grown in high altitude areas of Latin America, Eastern Africa, Asia, and Arabia, which contributes to their distinct flavors influenced by the specific climates and soil conditions of these regions. Because of their superior flavor, Arabica beans are generally more expensive and sought after in the specialty coffee market.

On the other hand, Robusta beans have a stronger, more bitter flavor with a higher caffeine content and are typically grown at lower altitudes in regions like West and Central Africa, Southeast

Asia, and Brazil. Robusta is less expensive and often used in espresso blends for added body and crema, and in instant coffee products due to its robust flavor.

The choice between Arabica and Robusta beans will affect a business's coffee profile, pricing strategy, and target market. Specialty coffee shops tend to favor Arabica for its nuanced flavors, while businesses focusing on stronger, more caffeine-rich coffees might opt for Robusta or blends.

Understanding the origins of coffee is equally crucial. Coffee beans are grown in the "Bean Belt," which includes countries like Brazil, the world's largest producer, known for its vast output of both Arabica and Robusta beans. Colombia, another major producer, is renowned for its high-quality Arabica coffee, often characterized by a mild, slightly nutty flavor. Ethiopian coffee, where Arabica originally hails from, is famous for its diverse and complex profiles, often floral and fruity, reflecting the indigenous varietals grown only in this region.

The provenance of coffee not only informs its taste but also its market value and sustainability considerations. Many coffee-producing regions face challenges such as climate change, economic instability, and social issues, which impact production and supply chains. Businesses must navigate these aspects by developing direct trade relationships with growers or through certified fair trade and organic suppliers to ensure ethical sourcing practices.

Sourcing and supply chain management in the coffee industry require a strategic approach where quality, cost, sustainability, and ethical practices are balanced. Establishing strong relationships with farmers and suppliers helps ensure a consistent quality of beans, fair pricing, and reliability in the supply chain. Moreover, transparency in sourcing can be a significant selling point, appealing to consumers increasingly interested in the ethical and environmental impacts of their purchases.

In summary, understanding the types and origins of coffee beans is more than just a matter of taste—it's a comprehensive strategy that influences purchasing decisions, supplier relationships, and ultimately, the success of a coffee business. This knowledge equips business owners to make informed choices that align with their brand's values and customer expectations, ensuring a sustainable and reputable operation in the competitive coffee market.

Building Relationships with Suppliers

Building strong relationships with suppliers is a fundamental aspect of starting and managing a successful coffee business. The quality of coffee served, the consistency of the product, and even the sustainability of the business heavily depend on these relationships. Establishing and maintaining good connections with coffee bean suppliers, equipment manufacturers, and other relevant parties can significantly influence both day-to-day operations and long-term growth.

For new coffee business owners, the first step in building these relationships is identifying the right suppliers. This involves researching and selecting those who not only offer quality products but also align with the business's values, such as ethical sourcing and environmental responsibility. Attending industry trade shows, joining coffee industry associations, and participating in online forums can provide valuable insights and connections that help in making informed decisions about suppliers.

Once potential suppliers are identified, the next step is to establish trust and mutual respect. This often starts with clear and transparent communication about your business goals, expected quality, and volume needs. Honest discussions about your business model and its alignment with the supplier's capabilities and ethical practices are crucial. For instance, if a coffee shop focuses on organic and fair-trade products, the owner should ensure the suppliers adhere to these standards.

Negotiating contracts that benefit both parties is also essential. These agreements should cover not only prices and delivery schedules but also quality standards and the flexibility to adjust orders based on demand changes. Flexibility can be particularly important for seasonal businesses or those in growth phases, as it allows the business to adapt without straining the relationship.

Maintaining the relationship involves regular communication and feedback sharing. Visiting suppliers, whether they are local farmers or international distributors, helps to strengthen the relationship and gives the business owner a better understanding of the production processes and challenges faced by the supplier. This understanding can lead to more effective collaboration and problem-solving when issues arise.

Furthermore, leveraging technology can enhance supply chain management by providing tools that offer real-time visibility into inventory levels, delivery statuses, and quality control. Advanced systems can help streamline ordering processes, predict demand more accurately, and manage payments efficiently, all of which can support a healthy relationship with suppliers.

Finally, recognizing and rewarding reliable suppliers can foster a long-term partnership. This could be through loyalty programs, longer contract terms, or even promoting the supplier's work as part of the coffee shop's marketing efforts. Highlighting a supplier's unique qualities or ethical practices can attract like-minded customers to the business, creating a win-win situation.

In conclusion, building relationships with suppliers in the coffee industry requires a strategic approach centered on mutual benefits, transparency, and consistent communication. By focusing on these elements, new coffee business owners can secure a supply chain that supports both the quality of their product and their company's values, setting a strong foundation for business success.

Sustainability in Sourcing

Sustainability in sourcing is a critical element for anyone starting a coffee business today, reflecting a growing consumer demand for ethically produced goods and the coffee industry's increasing awareness of its environmental and social impacts. Sustainable sourcing involves practices that are environmentally friendly, economically viable, and socially equitable, ensuring that the production processes contribute positively to the ecosystems and communities involved.

For a new coffee business, implementing sustainable sourcing practices begins with understanding the origins of coffee and the conditions under which it is grown. Coffee is primarily grown in the equatorial regions known as the Coffee Belt, where farming practices can have profound effects on local ecosystems. Sustainable sourcing emphasizes the importance of environmentally friendly practices, such as organic farming, which avoids the use of synthetic pesticides and fertilizers, and agroforestry, where coffee is grown under the canopy of trees, promoting biodiversity and soil health.

Economically, sustainable sourcing ensures that farmers receive a fair wage for their labor. This aspect is crucial because coffee farming is often characterized by volatility and low profit margins, which can lead to economic instability for farmers and their communities. Initiatives like Fair Trade and Direct Trade aim to address these issues by providing better earnings to farmers, improving their living conditions, and making the coffee supply chain more transparent. For a new coffee business, partnering with suppliers who follow these practices not only supports ethical business models but also resonates with consumers who are increasingly making purchasing decisions based on ethical considerations.

Social equity is another pillar of sustainable sourcing, focusing on improving labor conditions and providing social benefits to coffee-growing communities. This includes ensuring fair labor practices, access to healthcare, education, and avoiding child or forced labor. For coffee shop owners, this means choosing to source from farms and cooperatives that are known for their social responsibility towards their workers.

Moreover, sustainable sourcing also involves reducing the carbon footprint associated with coffee production and distribution. This can be achieved by optimizing supply chain logistics to decrease transportation distances and emissions, using sustainable packaging, and promoting recycling and composting practices both in the supply chain and in the coffee shop operations.

By integrating sustainability into the sourcing and supply chain management, new coffee business owners not only contribute to a more sustainable global coffee industry but also position their brand to appeal to a growing demographic of environmentally and socially conscious consumers. This strategic alignment not only helps protect the planet and support producer communities but also enhances the brand's reputation, potentially leading to increased customer loyalty and sales.

Implementing sustainable sourcing practices can be more complex and sometimes more costly than traditional methods, but it is a long-term investment in the health of the business and the global community. It involves educating oneself about the issues, communicating transparency in sourcing practices to customers, and being committed to continuous improvement in sustainability efforts. For those starting a coffee business, embracing these challenges as opportunities can set them apart in a competitive market and build a loyal customer base that values ethical and sustainable business practices.

Chapter 6: Branding and Marketing

Developing Your Brand Identity

Developing a brand identity is a crucial step for anyone starting a coffee business, as it distinguishes your cafe or coffee shop from competitors and forms a connection with your target audience. A strong brand identity encompasses the visual elements, the messaging, and the overall experience that your coffee business provides, all of which work together to communicate your business's values, personality, and promise to your customers.

At the core of developing your brand identity is defining what your coffee business stands for. This involves a deep understanding of your mission, vision, and the values you want to embody. Are you focusing on sustainability and ethically sourced beans? Do you pride yourself on artisanal techniques and specialty brews? Or is your coffee shop a community hub, a place for meetings and relaxation? Answering these questions will help you articulate your brand's personality and how it should be perceived by customers.

Once your brand's foundation is set, the next step is to translate this into a visual identity, which includes your logo, color scheme, typography, and other visual elements. These should reflect the personality and ethos of your brand. For instance, a coffee shop focusing on organic and sustainable practices might choose earth tones and a clean, minimalistic logo to convey its natural approach. The choice of typography, whether modern or classic, should also complement the overall feel of your brand.

In addition to visual elements, your brand identity should be evident through your messaging. This includes the language and tone used in your marketing materials, from your website to social media posts, as well as how your staff communicates with customers. Consistency in messaging reinforces your brand identity and helps build trust and recognition.

Your brand identity also extends to the atmosphere of your coffee shop. This encompasses the design and layout of your space, the music you play, the type of furniture you use, and even the style of your menu. Each element should contribute to the overall experience you want to create for your customers, making them feel a part of the story you are telling.

Marketing your brand effectively is equally important. Today's coffee shop patrons respond well to stories and experiences, not just products. Utilize social media to share the origins of your beans, the farmers you work with, or the process behind your coffee making. Engage with your community through events or collaborations with other local businesses. These strategies not only elevate your brand presence but also foster a community around your business.

Finally, consider the broader impact of your brand identity in your local and potentially global market. As the coffee industry is highly competitive, your brand needs to stand out by delivering a consistent, quality experience that customers can expect every time they visit your shop or order your products online.

By thoughtfully developing your brand identity and integrating it into every facet of your business, from your product offerings to your customer service, you can create a strong, recognizable brand that resonates with consumers and lays the groundwork for lasting success in the coffee industry.

Effective Marketing Strategies

Effective marketing strategies are vital for any new coffee business aiming to establish itself in a competitive market. These strategies encompass a broad range of activities focused on building a strong brand and reaching potential customers in impactful ways.

Creating a compelling brand identity is the cornerstone of marketing for a coffee business. This involves developing a distinctive logo, choosing an appealing color scheme, and crafting an overall aesthetic that resonates with the target audience. The brand identity should reflect the values and the unique selling proposition of the business—whether it's sustainability, premium quality, unique flavors, or community focus. This identity helps to differentiate the business from competitors and forms a connection with customers.

Storytelling is a powerful tool in branding. Sharing the origins of the coffee, the stories of the farmers, and the journey of the beans from the farm to the cup can create an engaging narrative that captivates consumers. These stories can be shared through packaging, online content, and in-store displays, fostering a deeper appreciation and loyalty among customers.

Digital marketing is increasingly important in the coffee industry, particularly social media marketing. Platforms like Instagram, Facebook, and Twitter provide opportunities to showcase the brand's personality, promote products, and interact directly with customers. High-quality visuals of the coffee shop, detailed photos of beverages, and behind-the-scenes content can attract followers and convert them into customers. Additionally, leveraging user-generated content, such as customer reviews and photos, can enhance credibility and attract new patrons.

Email marketing remains an effective strategy, especially for coffee shops looking to build and maintain customer relationships. Collecting emails through sign-ups—either in-store or online—allows businesses to send newsletters, promotions, and updates about new products or events, keeping the brand top-of-mind for consumers.

Local search engine optimization (SEO) is critical for coffee businesses, particularly those reliant on foot traffic. Optimizing the business's website and content for local keywords, maintaining an up-to-date Google My Business listing, and gathering positive online reviews are all strategies that enhance visibility in local search results, making it easier for potential customers to find the coffee shop when searching for nearby coffee options.

Collaborations and partnerships can also be an effective marketing approach. Partnering with local businesses or influencers who share similar target audiences can expose the brand to a broader audience. For instance, a coffee shop might collaborate with a local bookstore or bakery, offering cross-promotions that benefit both parties.

Finally, offering promotions and loyalty programs can be a great way to attract new customers and retain existing ones. Promotions such as "buy one, get one free," discounts for first-time visitors, or loyalty cards that offer a free drink after a certain number of purchases encourage repeat business and help build a loyal customer base.

In conclusion, effective marketing for a coffee business involves a mixture of traditional branding efforts, digital marketing, local SEO, and community engagement strategies. Each element plays a crucial role in building a strong brand presence and attracting both new and returning customers in a crowded marketplace.

Building a Customer Base

Building a customer base is pivotal for any new coffee business, as it not only establishes initial revenue streams but also fosters long-term sustainability and growth. The cornerstone of building a strong customer base lies in effective branding and strategic marketing that resonate with potential patrons and convert them into loyal customers.

The journey begins with developing a compelling brand identity. This encompasses your coffee business's name, logo, and the overall aesthetic of your physical or online presence. The aim is to create a visual and emotional representation that appeals to your target demographic. For a coffee business, this could mean adopting a modern, minimalist style to attract young professionals, or a warm, rustic decor that appeals to those seeking a cozy, community space. The key is consistency across all touchpoints, from your storefront to your website, ensuring that your brand identity is recognizable and memorable.

After establishing a strong visual identity, it's important to convey your brand's story and values. Today's consumers, especially millennials and Gen Z, prefer brands with authentic stories and ethical business practices. Whether it's your commitment to fair-trade coffee beans, environmentally friendly packaging, or community involvement, sharing these values can help forge deeper connections with customers who share similar beliefs.

Once your brand identity and values are in place, effective marketing strategies can bring your brand to life and attract customers. Digital marketing should be a primary focus, particularly leveraging social media platforms like Instagram, Facebook, and Twitter. These platforms allow you to visually showcase your products, share behind-the-scenes content, and engage directly with your audience through comments and messages. Additionally, targeted ads can help reach potential customers based on specific demographics, interests, and behaviors.

Content marketing is another powerful tool. Creating and sharing valuable content such as blogs about coffee brewing techniques, videos of your coffee sourcing trips, or newsletters featuring upcoming events can engage your audience and keep them informed. This not only establishes your expertise in the field but also builds a community around your brand.

Local search engine optimization (SEO) is crucial for coffee shops and local coffee roasteries. Ensuring your business is visible when potential customers search for coffee-related queries in your area can drive foot traffic. This involves optimizing your Google My Business listing and encouraging satisfied customers to leave positive reviews, which can improve your local search rankings and attract new customers.

Offline marketing strategies are equally important, especially for a location-based business. Participating in community events, offering coffee tastings, and collaborating with other local businesses can increase your visibility and attract a local clientele. Additionally, offering promotions, loyalty programs, and exceptional customer service can turn first-time visitors into regular customers.

Ultimately, building a customer base for a coffee business requires a blend of strong branding, digital prowess, community engagement, and consistent, quality service. By focusing on these elements, new coffee business owners can create a distinctive presence in the market, attract a dedicated following, and lay the foundation for lasting success.

Chapter 7: Operations Management

Daily Operations and Workflow

In the context of starting a coffee business, managing daily operations and workflow is critical to ensuring efficiency, customer satisfaction, and ultimately, profitability. Effective operations management involves overseeing all aspects of the coffee shop's daily activities, from opening routines to closing procedures, and everything in between.

The day typically begins before the doors even open. Staff arrive early to prepare the coffee shop for customers. This includes cleaning, setting up the service area, calibrating coffee machines, and preparing the first batch of fresh coffee. Ensuring that all equipment is in optimal condition is vital; a malfunctioning espresso machine can delay service and diminish the quality of the coffee.

Once the shop opens, the focus shifts to serving customers. Efficient workflow management is crucial here. Staff roles are clearly delineated to avoid overlaps and ensure smooth operations. For example, one employee might handle the cash register and customer greetings, another could manage coffee preparation, and a third might focus on food orders and cleanliness of the dining area. This division of labor helps maintain a flow where employees are not overburdened, and each has clear responsibilities.

Inventory management is an ongoing daily task. Staff need to monitor the levels of coffee beans, milk, sugar, pastries, and other supplies continuously. Running out of any item can lead to lost sales and dissatisfied customers. Therefore, effective inventory systems are put in place to track usage patterns and predict when restocking is necessary. Some sophisticated systems can automatically order stock when levels dip below a predetermined threshold.

Quality control is another critical component of daily operations. This involves not only the taste testing of coffee and food items to ensure consistency but also monitoring the presentation and speed of service. Regular training sessions help staff maintain high standards and introduce new menu items or brewing techniques, keeping the offerings fresh and engaging for regular customers.

In addition to these customer-facing activities, there are numerous back-office tasks that must be managed daily. These include bookkeeping, managing employee schedules, handling supplier interactions, and responding to customer feedback, especially on social media platforms. Modern coffee shops often use management software to streamline these processes, allowing owners and managers to focus more on strategic decisions rather than getting bogged down in day-to-day administration.

Customer service is woven through all these activities. Every interaction, whether it's taking an order, responding to a query, or resolving a complaint, contributes to the overall customer experience. Staff are trained to handle these interactions professionally and with a friendly demeanor that reflects the brand's values.

Closing procedures wrap up the day's activities. This includes cleaning the entire venue, turning off and cleaning the equipment, taking out the trash, and preparing the coffee shop for the next day. Reflecting on the day's sales, customer feedback, and any issues that arose helps in making necessary adjustments for future operations.

Effectively managing daily operations and workflow in a coffee business requires a balance between rigid efficiency and adaptive flexibility. This ensures not only that the business runs smoothly day-to-day but also adapts to longer-term changes in customer preferences and market conditions.

Staffing: Hiring and Training

Staffing is a critical component of operations management for any new coffee business, impacting everything from the daily workflow to the overall customer experience. Effective hiring and training can set a coffee shop apart in a competitive industry, ensuring that employees are not only skilled but also embody the culture and values of the business.

Hiring Process

The hiring process begins with identifying the specific roles needed to operate the coffee shop efficiently. These roles typically include baristas, kitchen staff, and possibly a manager if the owner is not handling day-to-day operations. Creating detailed job descriptions that outline responsibilities, required skills, and personal attributes can attract candidates who are a good fit for the coffee shop's culture and needs.

Once the roles are defined, promoting the job openings through various channels is crucial. Local job boards, social media platforms, and coffee industry forums can be effective. Additionally, leveraging networking within the coffee community can uncover passionate candidates who bring both skill and enthusiasm to their roles.

During the interview process, it is essential to assess not only the technical skills of the candidates, such as their ability to operate espresso machines and their knowledge of coffee brewing techniques, but also their soft skills. Customer service prowess, adaptability, and a passion for coffee are all traits that can indicate a candidate will contribute positively to the business.
Role-specific demonstrations, like a trial shift or a coffee-making test, can also provide practical insights into the candidate's capabilities and fit within the team.

Training Programs

Once the right team is in place, comprehensive training programs are essential to ensure consistent service and product quality. Training should cover not just the practical skills needed to perform job duties but also customer service, sales techniques, and an understanding of the business's values and vision.

Barista training is particularly important in a coffee shop. It should include:
- Coffee origins and types: Understanding the different beans and blends, their characteristics, and what makes them unique.
- Brewing techniques: Training on various equipment and methods, from espresso machines to manual brewers like French presses and Aeropresses.

- Drink preparation: Recipes and techniques for the full menu of offerings, including standard coffee drinks and specialty concoctions.
- Maintenance: Proper cleaning and maintenance of coffee machines and other equipment to ensure longevity and consistent quality of coffee.

For all staff, training should also emphasize the importance of customer interaction and how to handle busy periods with efficiency and calm. Engaging customers, managing orders with speed and accuracy, and dealing with complaints gracefully are all skills that enhance the customer experience and can create lasting loyalty.

Ongoing Development

Beyond initial training, encouraging ongoing development and continuous learning can help staff stay motivated and up-to-date with industry trends. Workshops, coffee tastings, and participation in barista competitions can be part of this. Regular performance reviews and feedback sessions also help staff understand their progress and areas for improvement, fostering a culture of transparency and continuous enhancement.

Retention Strategies

Finally, staff retention strategies are vital. Offering competitive wages, benefits, and a positive working environment can reduce turnover rates. Recognizing and rewarding employees for their hard work and dedication, whether through financial incentives, opportunities for advancement, or public acknowledgment, can also increase job satisfaction and loyalty.

In conclusion, staffing in the context of starting a coffee business involves strategic hiring and comprehensive training to build a team that not only performs well but also enhances the brand and contributes to a thriving business environment. Investing in people is as crucial as investing in quality coffee beans or equipment, as it is the staff who ultimately deliver the coffee experience to each customer.

Quality Control and Customer Service

Quality control and customer service are pivotal elements in the operations management of any coffee business, playing crucial roles in shaping customer satisfaction and loyalty. Ensuring consistent quality in every cup and providing exceptional service are not just about retaining customers, but also about carving out a reputation that can significantly boost the business's growth.

Quality control in a coffee business starts with the beans. It is vital to establish a relationship with reliable suppliers who provide high-quality coffee beans. This relationship is underpinned by regular tasting and testing to ensure that the beans meet specific flavor profiles and standards. This scrutiny extends to every step of the coffee-making process, from the grind of the beans to the temperature and timing of the water used. The goal is to produce a consistent product that customers can rely on every visit, which requires baristas who are well-trained and passionate about their craft.

The calibration of coffee machines and equipment is another critical factor in quality control. Regular maintenance and calibration ensure that the equipment performs optimally, delivering consistent taste and quality. This also involves periodic reviews and updates of the brewing techniques to adapt to new trends and improvements in coffee-making technology.

Alongside quality control, customer service forms the backbone of customer experience in a coffee business. Effective customer service starts the moment a customer enters the shop. Staff must be welcoming and knowledgeable, ready to answer any questions about the menu and to make recommendations based on customer preferences. Training staff to handle various customer interactions professionally and courteously can make a significant difference in how customers perceive the business.

Moreover, managing customer feedback is a critical aspect of customer service. Encouraging feedback, whether through direct conversations, comment cards, or online reviews, helps the business identify areas for improvement and create a responsive and customer-focused culture. Addressing complaints swiftly and effectively not only resolves individual issues but also shows that the business values its customers and is committed to continuous improvement.

Effective customer service also means creating an inviting atmosphere that makes customers want to return. This involves thoughtful interior design, comfortable seating, and considerate amenities like free Wi-Fi and power outlets. The ambiance should reflect the brand's identity and appeal to the target demographic.

Integrating technology can further enhance customer service. For instance, using a point-of-sale (POS) system that speeds up order processing and payment options is crucial for efficiency.

Additionally, a well-designed website and the use of social media can improve engagement and provide platforms for promotions and direct interaction with customers.

In conclusion, quality control and customer service are inseparable and essential parts of the operations management in a coffee business. They work together to deliver a product and experience that meets the expectations of today's discerning coffee lover. By focusing on these areas, a coffee business can differentiate itself in a competitive market, build a loyal customer base, and ensure long-term success.

Chapter 8: Scaling Your Business

Strategies for Growth and Expansion

Scaling a coffee business involves a series of strategic decisions and actions aimed at increasing its size, reach, and profitability. Successful growth and expansion are based on a foundation of understanding your current business operations, the market conditions, and the goals you aspire to achieve. Here are the key strategies for scaling a coffee business:

Diversification of Product Offerings: One effective strategy for growth is to diversify the products offered. This could include introducing new coffee blends or single-origin coffees that cater to different taste preferences. Expanding beyond coffee to include teas, smoothies, or locally sourced pastries can also attract a broader customer base. Seasonal or limited-time offers keep the menu exciting and encourage customers to visit more frequently.

Enhancing Customer Experience: Improving the customer experience is crucial for business growth. This can be achieved through faster service, more comfortable seating arrangements, and engaging with customers through loyalty programs. Offering Wi-Fi, hosting community events, or even providing live entertainment can create a more inviting atmosphere that encourages longer stays and more frequent visits.

Leveraging Technology: Technology can streamline operations and improve customer interactions. Implementing a point-of-sale (POS) system that handles inventory, sales, and customer data can help in making informed decisions about the business. Mobile apps for ordering and payment not only improve operational efficiency but also enhance the customer experience by reducing wait times.

Expanding Physical Locations: Opening new locations is a direct method of scaling your business. This requires thorough market research to identify areas with high foot traffic and a demographic likely to be interested in your offerings. A new location should align with the brand and the quality of the original to ensure consistency in customer experience.

Franchising: Franchising is a growth strategy that involves allowing other entrepreneurs to open their own locations under your brand name. This can rapidly expand the brand's presence and market reach without the need to manage each new location directly. However, it requires a strong brand identity and operational model that can be easily replicated.

Building an Online Presence: Developing an online presence extends the reach of the coffee business beyond its physical locations. An engaging website, active social media engagement, and digital marketing strategies can attract more customers.

Selling coffee products or merchandise online can also create additional revenue streams.

Sustainability Practices: Incorporating sustainable practices can not only reduce operational costs but also appeal to environmentally conscious consumers. This might involve sourcing coffee responsibly, using biodegradable cups, or implementing energy-saving practices in shops.

Partnerships and Collaborations: Collaborating with other businesses or local artists can create unique offerings and draw in new customers. Partnerships with local bakeries, dairy farms, or bookstores can enhance the product offerings and provide mutual benefits.

Staff Training and Development: As the business grows, ensuring that all employees uphold the quality and service standards is vital. Investing in training and development improves staff performance and motivation, which in turn enhances customer service and retains high-quality employees.

Each of these strategies requires careful planning and execution. It's important to monitor the outcomes of these strategies through feedback and performance metrics, adjusting the approach as needed to ensure continued growth and success in the competitive coffee industry.

Franchising Opportunities

Franchising offers a compelling pathway for scaling a coffee business by leveraging an established brand's name, operational model, and customer base. For entrepreneurs who have successfully established a coffee shop and are considering expansion, franchising can be an efficient strategy to grow their business while minimizing the direct management responsibilities typically associated with opening multiple locations.

At its core, franchising involves a legal and business relationship between the owner of the brand (the franchisor) and an individual or group (the franchisee) that wants to use the identity and business model of the franchisor to operate an independent location. This relationship is governed by a franchise agreement, which stipulates the terms of operation, the rights granted to the franchisee, and the obligations of both parties.

For the original coffee business owner, franchising serves as a method to expand the brand's footprint without the substantial capital investment required to open and operate new outlets directly. Instead, the franchisee typically bears the capital costs, including leasing or purchasing property, buying equipment, and other startup expenses. This arrangement not only reduces financial risks for the franchisor but also accelerates the pace of expansion.

However, successful franchising hinges on the transferability of the business model. The coffee shop must have a proven, replicable business model that can be easily duplicated in new locations. This includes consistent product quality, customer service, brand image, and operational procedures. To ensure uniformity across franchises, extensive training programs are essential. These programs cover everything from the preparation of coffee using specific methods and recipes, to customer service techniques, and day-to-day shop management.

Additionally, the franchisor must provide ongoing support to franchisees, which can include marketing assistance, regular quality checks, updates in business operations, and continuous training. This support helps maintain brand standards and ensures that each franchisee has the resources needed to succeed.

Marketing plays a critical role in the success of a franchised coffee business. The brand must already possess a strong, appealing image that can attract franchisees and customers alike. The franchisor should establish comprehensive marketing strategies that can be implemented locally by franchisees, while also promoting the brand at a national or international level to boost recognition and attract potential franchise buyers.

Another crucial aspect of franchising in the coffee industry is adapting to local markets while maintaining brand consistency. Each location may need to adjust its product offerings or store layout to better suit local preferences and behaviors, yet it should still be unmistakably part of the larger brand family.

For anyone considering franchising their coffee business, it's important to seek legal and business advice to develop a sound franchising agreement and strategy. Proper legal frameworks protect both the franchisor and the franchisees, and clear guidelines ensure the smooth operation of each franchise under the umbrella brand.

In conclusion, franchising offers a viable option for coffee shop owners to scale their operations efficiently. By focusing on a strong, transferable business model, comprehensive training, robust support systems, effective marketing, and adaptability to local markets, coffee business owners can successfully expand their presence and thrive in new markets through franchising.

Diversifying Your Product Offerings

Diversifying product offerings is a crucial strategy for scaling a coffee business and sustaining its growth in a competitive market. As customer preferences evolve and the market landscape shifts, expanding the range of products can help attract a broader customer base and increase revenue streams.

Initially, a coffee business might focus solely on serving high-quality coffee. However, to scale effectively, it should consider introducing a variety of related products and services that complement its core offerings. This could include different types of beverages, such as teas, specialty drinks, and seasonal specials that cater to diverse customer preferences. For instance, offering a selection of herbal teas or matcha can appeal to non-coffee drinkers and those interested in health-conscious alternatives.

Adding food items to the menu is another effective way to diversify. Simple pastries, sandwiches, and breakfast items can significantly enhance the coffee shop experience, encouraging customers to stay longer and spend more. Over time, more elaborate menu items like salads, soups, and desserts can be introduced, turning the coffee shop into a café that serves multiple meal periods.

Beyond consumables, coffee businesses can also explore retailing coffee-related products. Selling whole or ground coffee beans, especially those used in the shop, allows customers to enjoy their favorite coffee at home. This can be extended to branded merchandise such as mugs, t-shirts, and reusable cups, as well as coffee-making equipment like French presses, espresso machines, and grinders. These products not only provide additional revenue streams but also help in building the brand outside the shop.

Moreover, offering coffee subscriptions and gift packages can be an excellent way to generate recurring revenue. Subscriptions encourage repeat business by delivering coffee beans or grounds to customers on a regular basis, while gift packages can attract new customers, especially during holiday seasons or special events.

Workshops and classes on coffee brewing and appreciation are another avenue for diversification. These can engage the community, enhance the shop's reputation as a coffee authority, and create another revenue source. By educating customers on coffee origins, brewing techniques, and flavor profiles, a business can deepen customer loyalty and even attract a niche market interested in higher-end coffee experiences.

Expanding into online sales is an essential component of scaling a coffee business today. A robust online presence that allows customers to purchase coffee, merchandise, and even gift cards can dramatically extend the business's reach beyond local consumers to a national or even international audience.

Incorporating these diversified offerings requires thoughtful planning and execution. Each new product or service should align with the brand's identity and values. It's also important to consider the operational implications, including supply chain management, inventory, and staff training, to ensure the quality and service standards are maintained.

Through diversification, a coffee business can not only increase its profitability but also enhance its resilience against market fluctuations and changes in consumer behavior. This strategic expansion helps in maintaining relevance in the market, ensuring long-term growth and success.

Chapter 9: Financial Management

Managing Finances: Accounting Basics

Managing finances effectively is fundamental to the success of any business, especially in the competitive coffee industry. For entrepreneurs starting a coffee business, understanding accounting basics is crucial for maintaining healthy operations and supporting sustainable growth. This entails a meticulous approach to setting up financial systems, monitoring cash flows, and making informed business decisions based on financial data.

At the core of financial management in a coffee business is the setup of a reliable accounting system. This system serves as the backbone for tracking all financial transactions, including sales, expenses, payroll, and inventory costs. A good accounting software tailored to small businesses can automate many of these processes, allowing owners to maintain accurate records with less manual effort. The choice of software should align with the specific needs of the coffee shop, such as integration with point-of-sale (POS) systems, which can streamline sales tracking and inventory management.

One of the first tasks in managing finances is to differentiate between fixed and variable costs. Fixed costs, such as rent, utilities, and salaries, do not change with the level of business activity. Variable costs, like coffee beans, milk, and bakery items, fluctuate based on the volume of coffee sold. Understanding these costs is vital for pricing products correctly and forecasting future expenses.

Effective cash flow management is another critical aspect. Coffee businesses must regularly monitor their cash flow to ensure they have enough cash on hand to cover day-to-day operations. This involves careful timing of income and expenditures, managing supplier payments, and keeping a reserve for unexpected expenses. Proper cash flow management helps avoid financial strain, particularly in the early stages of the business when revenue might still be stabilizing.

Budgeting is also an essential tool in financial management. It involves creating a detailed plan for expected income and expenses over a specific period, usually monthly or quarterly. This budget should account for both the regular costs of running the coffee shop and one-time investments, such as purchasing new equipment or marketing campaigns. Regularly comparing actual financial results with the budget can help identify areas where the business is over or under-performing, allowing for timely adjustments.

Tax planning is another crucial element that coffee business owners need to manage proactively. Understanding the specific tax obligations, including sales tax, income tax, and payroll taxes, is necessary to comply with legal requirements and avoid penalties. Working with a professional accountant or tax advisor can provide valuable guidance in navigating complex tax laws and planning for tax liabilities effectively.

Finally, financial analysis is vital for understanding the overall financial health of the coffee business. Key financial ratios such as gross profit margin, net profit margin, and return on investment offer insights into profitability and operational efficiency. Regular analysis of these metrics can help business owners make informed decisions about expansions, cost-cutting, and strategic adjustments to their business model.

In conclusion, mastering the basics of financial management allows coffee shop owners to establish a stable financial foundation, optimize their operations, and pave the way for future growth. By diligently applying these principles, entrepreneurs can not only keep their business financially healthy but also position themselves favorably in the competitive coffee market.

Pricing Strategies

In the context of starting a coffee business, developing effective pricing strategies is crucial for ensuring profitability while staying competitive. A well-considered pricing strategy takes into account various factors such as cost, market demand, competitor pricing, and overall business goals.

First, understanding the cost structure is fundamental. This includes the direct costs associated with procuring coffee beans, milk, and other ingredients. It also involves indirect costs such as rent, utilities, labor, and equipment. A thorough cost analysis helps in setting a baseline price that covers all expenses while ensuring a profit margin. For coffee businesses, it's typical to mark up the cost of goods sold (COGS) by a certain percentage to achieve desired profitability.

Market-based pricing is another essential strategy where prices are set based on what customers are willing to pay, influenced by market demand and competitor pricing. This requires research into local coffee shop pricing and understanding the unique value proposition your coffee business offers. For instance, if your coffee shop offers a premium experience or unique coffee blends, you might price higher than a more conventional coffee shop.

Competitive analysis is integral to pricing strategy. Observing and analyzing the prices of competitors helps in positioning your offerings attractively. If competitors are pricing their products at a premium, entering the market at a slightly lower price can attract price-sensitive customers. Conversely, if your business offers superior quality or service, pricing higher can create a perception of luxury or exclusivity.

Value-based pricing focuses on the perceived value to the customer rather than just the cost of production. This strategy works well for businesses that offer specialty products, such as organic or single-origin coffees, which can command higher prices due to their perceived quality and the storytelling aspect of their marketing.

Psychological pricing tactics can also be effective. Setting prices just below whole numbers, like $2.99 instead of $3.00, often makes a price seem more attractive to consumers. Additionally, offering product bundles, like a coffee with a pastry at a combined lower price, can increase the perceived value and encourage more spending.

Pricing flexibility should be considered to adapt to changes in cost, competition, and consumer preference. Seasonal pricing for special flavors or holiday promotions, happy hour discounts, and loyalty programs are tactics that can keep pricing dynamic and engaging for customers.

Finally, transparency in pricing fosters trust and loyalty among customers. Clearly communicating why your products are priced a certain way, especially if they are higher than average, can reinforce the value customers are getting, whether it's supporting sustainable farming practices or enjoying a premium coffee experience.

Implementing these pricing strategies requires continuous monitoring and adjustment. Regularly reviewing costs, market conditions, and competitor actions will help the coffee business remain competitive and profitable in a dynamic market environment.

Profit Maximization Tips

Profit maximization in the coffee business is essential for sustainability and growth. Achieving this requires a keen understanding of both cost control and revenue enhancement while maintaining quality and customer satisfaction. Here are several strategies tailored specifically for coffee business owners to maximize their profits.

Cost Control

Effective cost management is the backbone of profit maximization. Begin by scrutinizing the cost of goods sold (COGS), which for a coffee shop primarily includes coffee beans, milk, sugar, and other consumables. Bulk purchasing or negotiating with suppliers for better rates can reduce these costs significantly without compromising quality. Additionally, managing inventory efficiently to avoid overstocking or understocking can prevent wastage and unnecessary expenses.

Labor costs are another significant expenditure in coffee shops. Optimizing staff schedules according to peak and non-peak hours ensures that you are not overstaffed during slow periods. Investing in training for your employees can also increase efficiency, thereby reducing the need for a larger staff while enhancing customer service.

Utility costs can be trimmed by adopting energy-efficient appliances and practices. From LED lighting to energy-efficient espresso machines and grinders, the upfront cost is often offset by the long-term savings in energy bills.

Revenue Enhancement

To enhance revenue, consider diversifying your product offerings. While coffee remains the centerpiece, offering a range of complementary products such as pastries, sandwiches, or even coffee-related merchandise can attract a broader customer base and increase average transaction sizes.

Seasonal and limited-time offerings can create buzz and draw in customers. Special holiday drinks, summer iced coffees, and unique blends can encourage customers to visit more frequently and try new products, thereby increasing sales.

Loyalty programs incentivize repeat customers and can significantly boost your revenue. A well-structured loyalty program not only encourages repeat business but also helps in collecting customer data that can be used for targeted marketing and personalized offers.

Efficient Pricing Strategies

Setting the right price is crucial. Analyze the pricing strategies of your competitors and consider your target market's spending habits. Psychological pricing techniques, such as pricing products just below whole numbers (e.g., $2.99 instead of $3.00), can also subtly enhance sales.

Dynamic pricing based on time of day or day of the week (happy hours, morning specials) can help in managing demand and maximizing profits during slower periods.

Leveraging Technology

Adopting the right technology can streamline operations and enhance customer experiences, leading to higher sales and lower costs. Point-of-sale (POS) systems can expedite order processing and improve inventory management. Digital platforms for online orders and mobile payments can also open up new revenue streams and meet the preferences of tech-savvy customers.

Marketing and Customer Engagement

Effective marketing drives visibility and customer engagement. Utilize social media platforms to showcase your products, share positive customer testimonials, and announce special promotions. Engaging with customers through these platforms can also provide valuable feedback and build a community around your brand.

Creating a welcoming ambiance in your coffee shop can enhance customer experiences and encourage longer stays and higher spending. Free Wi-Fi, comfortable seating, and a pleasant interior design can make your coffee shop a destination rather than just a quick stop.

By implementing these strategies, coffee business owners can maximize their profits through careful management and innovative growth tactics. Each element, from cost management to marketing, plays a crucial role in building a successful and profitable coffee business.

Chapter 10: Navigating Challenges

Handling Competition

Handling competition is a critical aspect of navigating the challenges of starting and operating a coffee business. In a market that is as saturated and diverse as the coffee industry, understanding how to differentiate oneself and maintain a competitive edge is vital for survival and growth.

In the coffee business, competition comes from various fronts: large chains with significant marketing budgets, local artisan cafes with loyal followings, and even non-traditional outlets like fast-food restaurants and supermarkets offering coffee options. To thrive in this competitive landscape, a new coffee business needs to adopt several strategic approaches.

First and foremost, defining a unique selling proposition (USP) is crucial. This involves identifying what makes your coffee shop or product stand out. Whether it's a unique brewing method, a commitment to sustainability, exceptional customer service, or a cozy ambiance, your USP should resonate with your target audience's preferences and values. For example, a coffee shop might focus on organic and fair-trade coffee beans, appealing to environmentally conscious consumers.

Understanding the local market is another key strategy. By conducting thorough market research, business owners can identify gaps in the market or underserved locations. This could involve opening a shop in an area with high foot traffic but few coffee shops or offering products that aren't available elsewhere in the market, such as exotic blends or specialty drinks.

Building a strong brand is also vital in handling competition. Effective branding extends beyond logos and interior design; it encompasses the entire customer experience. This means training staff to deliver consistently friendly service, creating a memorable and comfortable atmosphere, and maintaining quality across all aspects of the business. A strong brand builds customer loyalty, which is crucial in a competitive market.

Leveraging technology can provide a competitive advantage as well. This includes adopting the latest in coffee brewing technology to enhance product quality or using customer relationship management (CRM) software to personalize customer interactions and create targeted marketing campaigns. Additionally, having a robust online presence through social media and an attractive, user-friendly website can help attract new customers and engage existing ones.

Collaborations and partnerships can also be effective in mitigating competition. Partnering with local businesses or community events can increase visibility and attract a broader customer base. For instance, a coffee shop could host local art exhibits or music nights, providing a community space that offers more than just coffee. Such initiatives not only draw in customers but also create a community hub that differentiates the business from typical coffee shops.

Finally, constant innovation in products and services can keep the business relevant and exciting to customers. This could mean regularly updating the menu, introducing seasonal offerings, or even providing workshops and classes on coffee appreciation and brewing techniques. Continuous improvement and adaptation to customer feedback and industry trends will keep the business dynamic and competitive.

In conclusion, handling competition in the coffee industry requires a multifaceted approach that includes understanding the market, differentiating the business through a strong USP and branding, leveraging technology, fostering community relationships, and continually innovating. These strategies, when executed effectively, can help a new coffee business not only survive but thrive amidst a crowded and competitive marketplace.

Crisis Management

Crisis management is a critical component for any business, especially for startups in the highly competitive coffee industry. When starting a coffee business, entrepreneurs must be equipped with strategies to handle unexpected challenges that could threaten their operation, reputation, and financial stability. Effective crisis management involves preparation, swift action, and clear communication, all aimed at mitigating risks and maintaining business continuity.

For coffee businesses, crises can come in various forms, such as supply chain disruptions, health and safety incidents, economic downturns, or public relations issues. Each type of crisis demands a tailored response strategy that addresses the immediate concerns while also safeguarding the long-term interests of the business.

Preparation is the first line of defense against crises. This includes developing a comprehensive crisis management plan that identifies potential risks specific to the coffee industry, such as crop failures, fluctuations in global coffee prices, or issues with food safety. The plan should outline clear procedures for responding to different scenarios, designate crisis management teams, and establish communication channels for internal and external stakeholders. Regular training and drills can help ensure that staff are familiar with the plan and can act effectively under pressure.

Swift action is crucial once a crisis hits. For a coffee shop, this might involve immediate measures to address a health scare, such as a foodborne illness linked to a product sold in the cafe. The business might need to halt sales, issue recalls, or close the shop temporarily to prevent further risk to customers. In the case of a supply chain disruption, the business may need to quickly find alternative suppliers to keep operations running without compromising the quality of the coffee served.

Clear communication is essential during a crisis to manage perceptions and maintain trust with customers, employees, and other stakeholders. This involves transparently sharing what is known about the situation, what is being done to resolve it, and what steps are being taken to prevent future occurrences. Effective communication not only helps to minimize damage to the brand but also reinforces the business's commitment to its values and responsibilities.

In addition to these responsive strategies, coffee businesses can benefit from a proactive approach to crisis management. This includes building strong relationships with suppliers and other partners to ensure mutual support in times of need. Diversifying suppliers and products can also reduce the risk of severe impact from any single point of failure.

Financial resilience is another crucial aspect of crisis management. Maintaining healthy cash reserves, having access to credit, and planning for financial contingencies can provide the buffer needed to weather periods of reduced business activity without making drastic cuts to operations or workforce.

Lastly, learning from past crises is invaluable. After navigating a challenging period, coffee business owners should review their response—what worked, what didn't, and what could be improved. This review process should be a continuous part of the business's approach to crisis management, adapting the plan to better handle any future crises.

By incorporating these strategies into their business practices, coffee shop owners can not only manage crises more effectively but also position their businesses to recover and thrive post-crisis. This resilience can become a competitive advantage, demonstrating reliability and commitment to quality and safety that can attract and retain customers even in the most challenging times.

Adapting to Market Changes

Adapting to market changes is a critical skill for any entrepreneur, especially in the dynamic world of coffee businesses. As consumer preferences shift, technology evolves, and economic factors fluctuate, staying agile and responsive can make the difference between thriving and merely surviving.

The coffee industry, like many others, is subject to rapid changes in consumer behavior. For instance, recent years have seen a surge in demand for sustainable and ethically sourced coffees. Customers are more informed and concerned about where their coffee comes from, how it is grown, and the impact of its production on the environment and local communities. Coffee shop owners must respond by ensuring their offerings align with these ethical considerations, potentially sourcing beans from fair-trade certified growers or investing in direct relationships with farms.

Technology also dramatically influences how coffee businesses operate. From the popularity of mobile ordering apps to the implementation of advanced point-of-sale systems that streamline operations and enhance customer service, technology can not only help coffee shop owners manage their businesses more efficiently but also provide a richer customer experience. For example, by utilizing data analytics, shop owners can track consumer behavior patterns, adjust their menus, and optimize staffing schedules based on predicted busy times.

Economic changes are another area where adaptability is crucial. Factors such as fluctuations in coffee bean prices due to global supply issues or changes in local economic conditions can impact profitability. Successful coffee shop owners monitor these trends closely and adjust their pricing strategies, procurement processes, or even menu offerings in response to changing economic conditions to maintain their margins.

Moreover, the competitive landscape in the coffee industry can change quickly. New entrants, innovative products, or shifts in consumer loyalty can all threaten an established business's market share. To stay competitive, coffee shop owners need to continuously innovate and differentiate their offerings. This could mean experimenting with new flavors and products, enhancing the customer experience, or leveraging marketing strategies that emphasize unique aspects of their business, such as community involvement or local partnerships.

Lastly, adaptability is not just about responding to external changes but also about anticipating them. This proactive approach involves staying informed about industry trends, engaging with customers to solicit feedback and ideas, and even looking beyond the coffee industry to identify emerging trends that could be translated into the coffee business context.

In sum, adapting to market changes requires a combination of keen observation, ongoing engagement with customers and community, strategic use of technology, and a willingness to innovate continuously. For those starting a coffee business, building adaptability into their business plan from the outset can provide a strong foundation for long-term success.

Chapter 11: The Future of Coffee Business

Innovations in Coffee

Innovations in the coffee industry are transforming how businesses operate, from bean to cup, and understanding these changes is crucial for anyone looking to start a coffee business. The landscape is continuously evolving, driven by technological advancements, consumer expectations, and the pursuit of sustainability.

One of the most significant innovations in the coffee industry is the advancement in coffee brewing technology. Automated espresso machines and single-serve coffee makers have revolutionized coffee shops and homes, offering consistency and convenience without sacrificing quality. High-tech machines now mimic the techniques of expert baristas, ensuring that every cup of coffee is perfectly brewed. This technology not only improves efficiency and customer satisfaction but also reduces the need for highly skilled labor, allowing business owners to manage costs more effectively.

Another innovation reshaping the coffee industry is the application of blockchain technology for traceability and transparency. Consumers increasingly demand to know the origin of their coffee and the conditions under which it was produced. Blockchain allows coffee businesses to provide a transparent supply chain from farmer to consumer, ensuring that the beans are ethically sourced and farmers receive fair compensation. This level of transparency not only appeals to ethically conscious consumers but also enhances the brand's reputation and customer loyalty.

Sustainability is also a major focus of innovation in the coffee industry. As environmental concerns become more prominent, coffee businesses are exploring new ways to reduce their ecological footprint. This includes everything from biodegradable packaging and recycling programs to investing in sustainable farming practices. Some companies are developing new agricultural techniques that increase yields and reduce water usage, helping to combat the effects of climate change on coffee production.

The rise of specialty coffees is another innovation area. Consumers' palates are becoming more sophisticated, driving demand for specialty and gourmet coffees with unique flavor profiles. Roasters and cafes are experimenting with different roasting techniques and bean varieties to cater to this demand. Additionally, the cold brew and nitro coffee trends have introduced new ways to experience coffee, offering smoother and richer flavors that appeal to a younger demographic.

Digital innovation is also pivotal in the coffee industry. From mobile ordering apps to loyalty programs, technology is used to enhance the customer experience and streamline operations. Social media platforms have become vital tools for marketing and customer engagement, allowing businesses to reach a wider audience and build a community around their brand. Moreover, e-commerce has enabled coffee businesses to sell their products online, reaching customers beyond their geographical location and increasing their sales potential.

For anyone starting a coffee business today, staying abreast of these innovations can provide a competitive edge. Incorporating cutting-edge technology, embracing sustainability, and responding to consumer trends are not just optional; they are essential strategies for success in the modern coffee industry. By leveraging these innovations, new coffee business owners can position themselves as forward-thinking and adaptable, key qualities for thriving in this dynamic market.

The Role of Technology

In the context of starting a coffee business, understanding the role of technology is crucial for staying competitive and innovative. The coffee industry, like many others, is undergoing a significant transformation driven by technological advancements that affect every stage of the coffee journey—from bean to cup.

At the farming level, technology is reshaping the way coffee is grown. Precision agriculture, which includes the use of drones and IoT (Internet of Things) sensors, enables farmers to monitor crop health, soil quality, and water usage more accurately. This data-driven approach helps in optimizing coffee plant yields and quality, ensuring that businesses can offer a consistently superior product. For new entrants into the coffee industry, partnering with farms that employ these technologies can be a strong selling point and a basis for a sustainable sourcing strategy.

When it comes to the processing and roasting stages, automation and AI are becoming increasingly prevalent. Automated roasting machines can now precisely control temperature and timing, reducing the reliance on manual labor and minimizing human error. This ensures a uniform roast, crucial for maintaining flavor consistency across batches. For startups in the coffee sector, investing in or utilizing these technologies can enhance production efficiency and consistency, key factors in building customer trust and satisfaction.

At the retail level, technology enhances the customer experience and streamlines operations. Digital point-of-sale (POS) systems, for example, not only handle transactions but also integrate inventory management, customer relationship management (CRM), and analytics. These systems provide coffee shop owners with valuable insights into consumer behavior, product performance, and business trends, enabling them to make informed decisions quickly. Additionally, mobile apps and loyalty programs, driven by technology, can foster a stronger connection between the business and its customers by offering convenience and personalized experiences.

Furthermore, the adoption of online sales channels is now a necessity rather than an option. E-commerce platforms allow coffee businesses to reach a broader audience, selling beans, coffee equipment, and merchandise beyond geographical limitations. This digital expansion is crucial for growth, especially in a world where consumers value the convenience of home delivery.

Lastly, technology also plays a vital role in sustainability—an increasingly important consideration in the coffee industry. Blockchain, for instance, can be used to enhance traceability and transparency in the coffee supply chain. This technology allows businesses and consumers to verify the origins of their coffee, ensuring it is ethically sourced and sustainably produced. For a new coffee business, promoting this level of transparency can significantly enhance brand credibility and appeal, especially among environmentally and socially conscious consumers.

For anyone starting a coffee business today, integrating technology into their business plan is not just an enhancement—it's essential. It positions the business for efficiency, growth, and a better understanding of the rapidly changing market dynamics and consumer preferences. Engaging with these technological tools and strategies can differentiate a startup from its competitors, creating a foundation for success in a crowded marketplace.

Predictions and Preparations for Future Trends

As the coffee industry continues to evolve, staying ahead of future trends and preparing for them is essential for anyone entering the market. The future of the coffee business is likely to be shaped by several key factors including sustainability, technology integration, changing consumer behaviors, and innovative business models.

Sustainability is expected to move from a niche concern to a central focus in the coffee industry. As environmental awareness grows among consumers, coffee businesses will need to prioritize eco-friendly practices across their operations. This includes everything from sourcing beans from farms that use sustainable growing practices to implementing energy-efficient methods in roasting and brewing, and even using biodegradable packaging. Additionally, businesses will increasingly need to demonstrate transparency in their supply chains, perhaps adopting blockchain technology to provide consumers with traceable coffee origins and production methods.

Technology will continue to transform the coffee landscape, especially in enhancing the customer experience and streamlining operations. Advanced espresso machines and brewing equipment that can consistently produce high-quality coffee are becoming more common. Furthermore, the use of artificial intelligence for personalized marketing, customer service chatbots, and predictive analytics in inventory management can help coffee shops better understand and anticipate customer needs and preferences.

Changing consumer behaviors will also dictate the evolution of the coffee industry. For instance, the rise of remote work could influence the location and design of coffee shops, as there may be a shift from city-center locations to neighborhood cafes that cater to telecommuters seeking a third space. Additionally, the demand for healthier options might lead to an increase in offerings like coffee blended with superfoods, organic selections, and alternatives to traditional dairy products.

Innovation in business models is another area where future trends are likely to emerge. Subscription services for coffee delivery, partnerships with non-coffee businesses, and seasonal pop-up cafes are just a few examples that can offer new revenue streams and diversification. Coffee businesses may also explore more collaborative models, such as co-roasting spaces where small roasters share resources to reduce costs and boost community engagement.

To prepare for these trends, new coffee business owners should consider building flexibility into their business plans to allow for adaptation to changing market conditions and consumer preferences. Investing in training and technology that can improve environmental performance and operational efficiency will also be crucial. Furthermore, networking with other industry professionals and staying engaged with industry news can provide insights and opportunities for innovation.

By anticipating these trends and preparing strategically, aspiring coffee business owners can position themselves to thrive in a future where change is the only constant, ensuring their venture remains relevant and successful in the evolving landscape of the coffee industry.

Conclusion

In concluding a guide on how to start a coffee business, it's important to reflect on the journey that prospective coffee shop owners are about to embark upon. Starting a coffee business is not just about selling coffee; it's about crafting an experience, building a community, and navigating the intricacies of a dynamic industry.

Firstly, the path to opening a coffee shop involves meticulous planning and dedication. As we've seen, understanding the market, identifying your niche, and creating a solid business plan are foundational steps that set the tone for the entire venture. Each decision, from choosing the location to selecting coffee suppliers, plays a critical role in shaping the business.

Moreover, financial planning cannot be overstressed. A new coffee business must manage its finances wisely to sustain operations and grow. This involves not only securing initial funding but also maintaining a keen eye on cash flow management, pricing strategies, and cost-effective marketing.

The human element of the coffee business is equally crucial. Hiring the right team, training them effectively, and maintaining a positive workplace culture are essential for providing exceptional service. After all, the staff are the face of your business and play a significant role in building customer loyalty.

Innovation and adaptability are key traits that will serve coffee business owners well. The coffee industry is ever-evolving, influenced by changes in consumer preferences, technological advancements, and economic shifts. Staying informed and flexible allows business owners to pivot strategies as needed, ensuring longevity and relevance in a competitive market.

Finally, the importance of passion and perseverance cannot be overstated. Starting and running a coffee business is a journey filled with challenges, but it also offers immense rewards. From the joy of crafting the perfect brew to the satisfaction of creating a beloved local spot, the personal fulfillment that comes with this venture is profound.

To prospective coffee shop owners: armed with knowledge, preparation, and enthusiasm, you are well-equipped to enter the world of coffee. Remember that each cup of coffee you serve carries your signature and represents your commitment to quality and community. Embrace the journey, anticipate challenges, and enjoy the process of creating a space where coffee and culture meet.

www.ingramcontent.com/pod-product-compliance
Lightning Source LLC
Chambersburg PA
CBHW032211220526
45472CB00018B/1101